Contents

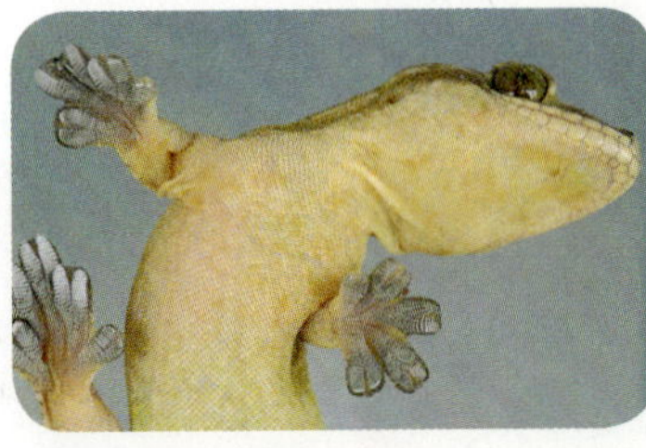

Chapter 1

Meet the Reptiles

Amazon tree boa

See this sleek and slithering snake? Do you know what kind of animal it is? The answer is a reptile!

See the long backbone in this snake skeleton?

Snakes are not slimy. They are covered in dry scales that look like this close up.

How can you tell if something is a reptile? All reptiles have skin that is dry and scaly. All reptiles are also **vertebrates**. That means they have backbones.

Fast Fact

Reptiles are cold-blooded. They cannot make their own body heat like mammals and birds can. Reptiles lie in the sun to stay warm.

The world is filled with many different kinds of reptiles. There are snakes. There are lizards.

There are turtles and tortoises. There are alligators and crocodiles, too. Let's learn more about these really cool creatures!

Chapter 2

Reptile Skills

tokay gecko

Reptiles are great at getting around! This lizard can run straight up a slick piece of glass.

Reptiles	What They Eat
snakes	mice, lizards, birds, eggs
lizards	plants, insects, birds, mammals
turtles	plants, fish, worms, insects
tortoises	plants, fruit, flowers, insects
alligators	fish, frogs, snakes, birds
crocodiles	fish, turtles, birds, mammals

chameleon

Reptiles are excellent hunters. Chameleons use their long tongues to snatch tasty insects. ZAP!

Can you see the gecko hiding on this tree?

Some reptiles are great at **blending** in with their surroundings. This helps them to hide from hungry predators.

Some reptiles have other tricks for staying safe. Box turtles hide in their shells. Hognose snakes turn upside down and pretend to be dead.

Chapter 3

Amazing Reptiles

A scientist shows off her pet anaconda.

Say hello to a VERY big snake called an anaconda. Some of them grow to be 35 feet long. That is as long as a school bus!

Fast Fact

The pygmy chameleon is minuscule. It's so tiny it can fit on a fingertip!

Komodo dragon

Check out the world's largest lizard. It can eat 100 pounds of food in one meal. That is like gobbling down 400 hamburgers!

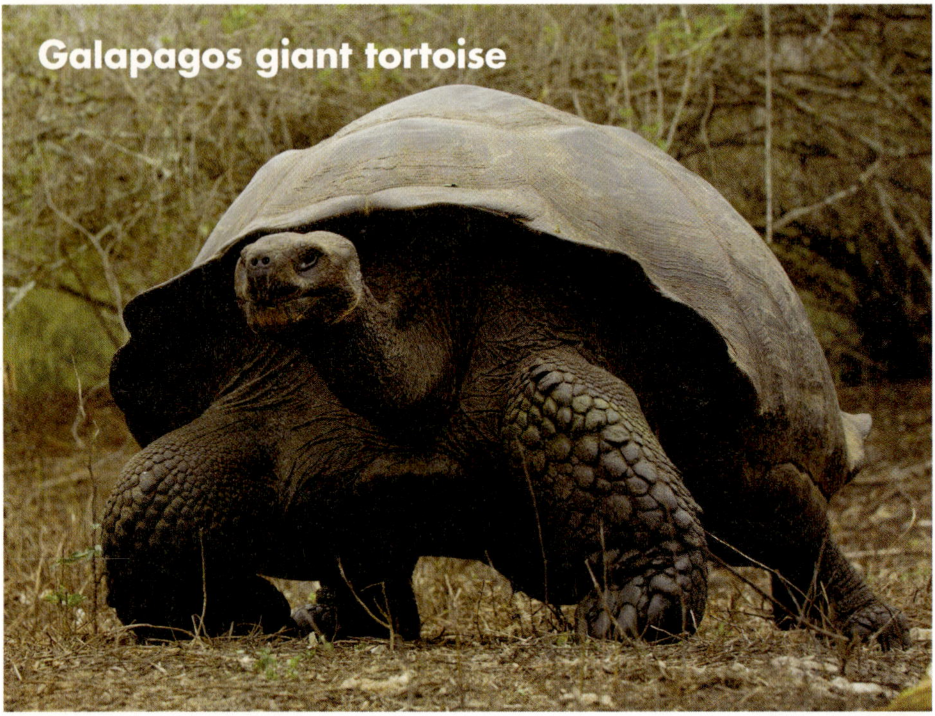
Galapagos giant tortoise

Fast Fact

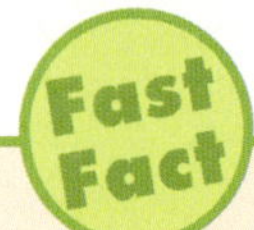

Tortoises live on land.
Turtles live mostly in water.

Tortoises can live for more than 150 years! That is older than any other reptile. In fact, that is older than any other land animal.

alligator

Some alligators can go a whole year without eating. They **conserve** energy by hardly moving at all. Wow! See you later, alligator!

Glossary

blend (**blend**): to mix in with the background

cold-blooded (**kohld-bluhd**-id): having a body temperature that changes according to the surrounding temperature

conserve (kuhn-**surv**): to save

minuscule (**min**-uh-skule): very tiny

scales (**skales**): the small pieces of hard skin that cover the body of a reptile or fish

species (**spee**-sheez): a group of animals or plants that share the same characteristics

vertebrates (**vur**-tuh-brates): animals that have backbones

Comprehension Questions

1. Can you share two things that make a reptile a reptile?
2. Can you name five animals that are reptiles?
3. Which reptile in this book is your favorite? Tell why.